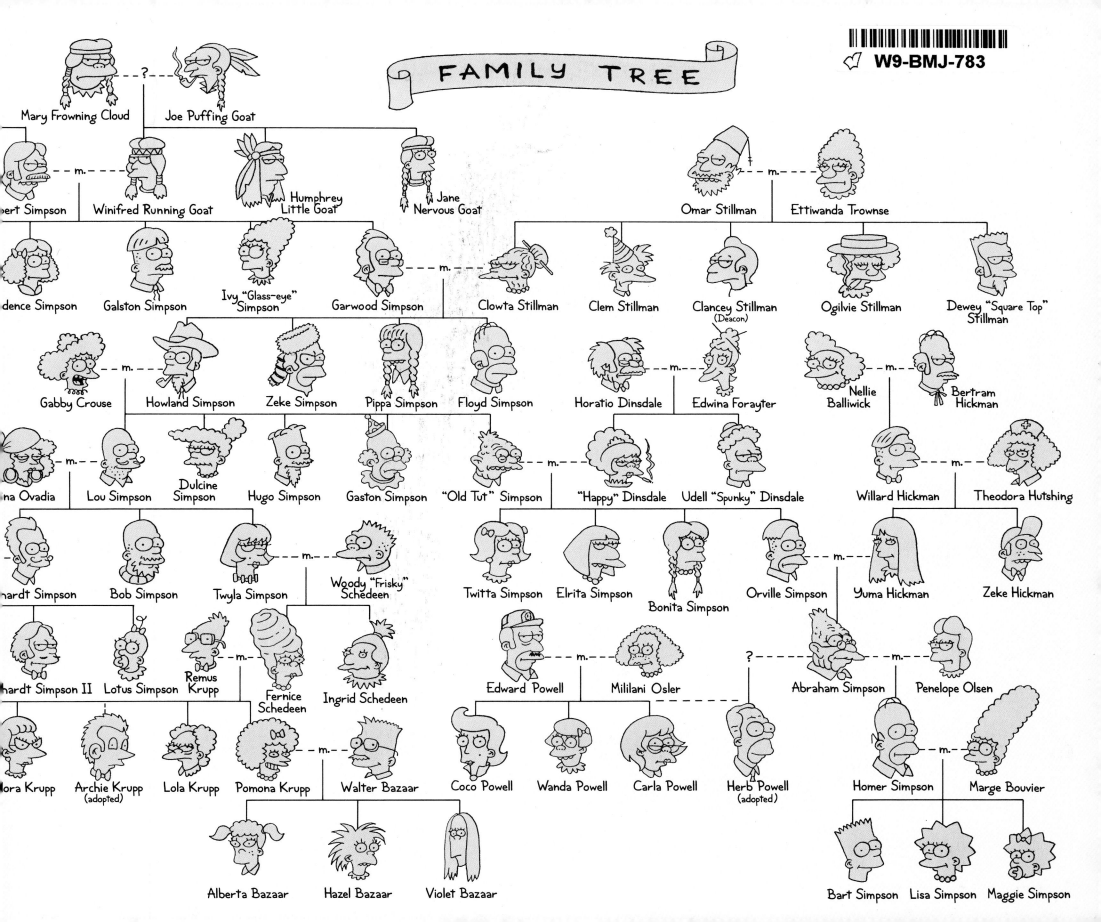

FAMILY TREE

Dedicated to the memory of Snowball I:

We've re-upholstered the couch you shredded, but not our love for you.

THE SIMPSONS™ UNCENSORED FAMILY ALBUM.

Copyright © 1991 by Matt Groening Productions, Inc. All rights reserved. Printed in Mexico. No part of this book may be used or reproduced in any manner whatsoever without written permission except in the case of brief quotations embodied in critical articles and reviews. For information, address HarperCollins Publishers, 10 East 53rd Street, New York, NY 10022.

FIRST EDITION

ISBN 0-06-096582-7

91 92 93 94 95 RRD 10 9 8 7 6 5 4 3 2 1

Concepts and Art Direction: Mili Smythe   Family Album Chroniclers: Mary Trainor, Ted Brock
Design: Peter Alexander   Design Associate: Barbara McAdams   Production Assistance: Kim Llewellyn, Dan Chavira
Creative Team: John Adam, Dale Hendrickson, Ray Johnson, Bill "Babe" Morrison, Willardson & Associates.
Chronicle Contributor: Jamie Angell   Editor: Wendy Wolf   Legal Advisor: Susan Grode
Typesetting: Skil-Set Graphics

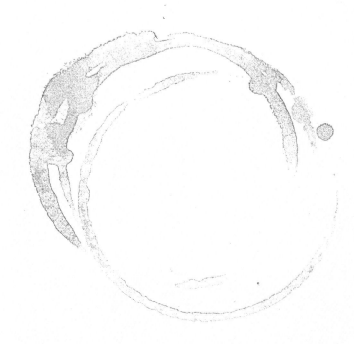

MATT GROENING'S

tHe SIMPSONS™

Uncensored Family Album

Harper Perennial
A division of HarperCollins Publishers

Great Grandma Bouvier, in her flapper days

Great Grampa Bouvier, right before he shipped out with the Merchant Marines. My grandmother once told me the song "Brandy" was based on his life.

To Pepe— For what it's worth— Bambi

Dr. Bouvier's FLESHWORM & BLACKHEAD ERADICATOR $1.00

↑ One of my Great-great Uncle Charlemagne's "Get-Rich-Quick" Schemes

Bouvier Family Picnic, 1903

Great Grandma Bouvier's dog, Fetchy.

Patty, Selma and me

Patty and Selma in their infancy, with our cat, Squirmy.

Patty, Selma (age 3½) and Squirmy.

My first book! In the end, the Li'l Gnome grows to be 9 ft. tall. It taught me a valuable lesson about patience, hope and growth!

My first tooth

My second tooth

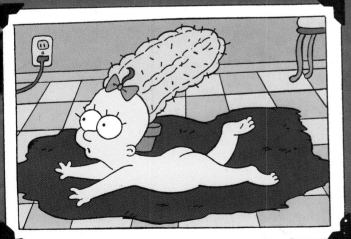

Little Marjorie Bouvier

OOH-WEE!

Despite my handicap, I won the kindergarten apple-bobbing contest.

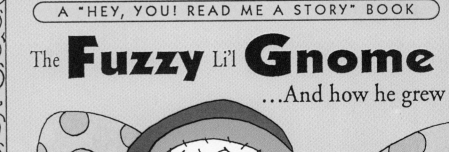

A "HEY, YOU! READ ME A STORY" BOOK

The Fuzzy Li'l Gnome

...And how he grew

Before ↓

After ↓

to Marge

Your pal, Bruce

My first boyfriend, Bruce Udelhofen

The day I straightened my hair (age 13).

The Speech I Imagine JFK Would Have Made
At Our Graduation (Had He Lived)

My fellow citizens of Springfield High, the trumpet
summons us again to a long twilight struggle. THe
torch has been passed to your generation and the
glow from that fire can truly light the campus.

So let us Begin.

Ich bin ein Springfielder!

    AXXWXXXX   Ask not what you can do for Spring-
field High, but what Springfield High can do for you..

Other way around ?

The first draft of my award-winning dramatic interpretation

Springfield High School

Certificate of Distinction

Awarded to: _____Marge Bouvier_____

In recognition of: _"Johnny, We Hardly Heard Ye"_

In the Category: _Dramatic Interpretation_

2ⁿᵈ Place   FORENSICS TEAM

Christina Marcello
Supervisor, Springfield School District

Seymour Skinner
Principal, Springfield High School

Artie Ziff took first place with his poignant reading of "Don't Rain on My Parade", from "Funny Girl."

All filled in! February 23, 1945 - Iwo Jima

Grandma and Grandpa Simpson's wedding.

I have them to thank for my dear Homer.

I found this in an old Almanac that Grandpa left in the bathroom.

12) PFC. Harris
13) Sgt. Mulrooney
15) Extinct species of N. American shrubbery
16) Former Yugoslavian unit of currency
17) What Generals do in battle
19) _____ mobile
23) _____ Manchu
24) S. American tree fungus
25) Imitated
27) Jap
30) PFC. Richards
31) Lt. Richards
32) Two-toed Eurasian marsupial
34) PFC. Winoski

DOWN
1) Tasmanian flowering ragweed-(2 words)

11) PFC. O'Ryan
14) PFC. Di Nunzio
18) The entire 23rd platoon_____
20) Popular tune

21) Chinese root weevil
22) Nip

25) PFC. Roberts
26) Sgt. Gitman
33) "Stars _____ Stripes"

YOU SHOWED UP

to Abe-baby XOX

I don't know what her name was, but I do know that Homer's once-wealthy half-brother, Herb, was the result of their short-lived affair.

Springfield Shopper
314 Dutch Elm St.
Springfield

Dear Shopper Editor,

I/¢ have had it up to here with your "news-
paper" and it's reckless, anti-social policy
of publishing story afterstory of babies
being born, picture after picture of babies,
advertisements of baby products, etc.

Where will it all end?

What about the rest of us who aren't not babies?
Did it ever occur to you that we are the
majority? If you ask me, you are only getting
yourself in a real mess because the people
will see all these babby stories and think
"That's a good way to get my name in the
paper," and that only leads to more babies!

So I'm ware warning you: if you continue this
policy, I will see to it that no child of
mine ever lays an eye on your publication.

Sicnerely,

Abraham Simpson

Abraham Simpson

P.S. If you don't think I'm serious, you
should see my newborn son. He shows no
interest in what your paper, or anything else
for that matter, has to say. More power to
him if you ask me!

Grandpa's first-recorded letter
of complaint

Little Homer
Simpson, age
3 months

Grandpa's 7,587th
oyster ↓

Homer always did have a fondness for donuts.

Grandpa and Homer in happier days.

The first sign of Homer's budding intelligence. I can't really say his handwriting has improved much over the years.

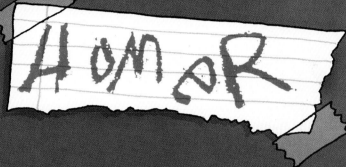

The happier days were over quite quickly.

SPRINGFIELD ELEMENTARY

"We mold young minds."

--Douglas Crone,
Ed D., Superintendent

Est. 1914

REPORT CARD

Simpson, Homer GRADE 4

SUBJECT	1ST QUARTER	2ND QUARTER	3RD QUARTER	4TH QUARTER	SUMMER-SCHOOL
MATH	D	D	D-	D-	F
ENG	D+	D	D-	F+	F
HIST	D	D+	D+	D-	F
SCI	D-	D-	F	D-	F
GYM	C-	C-	D	D+	D-
ATTEN-DANCE	F	D-	F	D-	F
CITIZEN-SHIP	F	D-	D-	F	D-

NOTES ~~We would like to hold Homer back a year, but his 4th grade teacher, Mrs. Harvell, has refused to take him back~~ —HH

an insult to ... disruption ... "underachie...

Our only photo of Herb Powell, Homer's once-wealthy half-brother.

Dear Principal Hartly,
Please excuse Homer's absince of Nov. 8-10. He had to stay home to look after his fathre, who was nearly blinded when he reached to a high shelf and took down a bottle of cleanser he was going to use to clean his medal for the Veterins Day Parade and the cleansr spilled in his face.
Signed,

HOMER'S DAD

Homer on Halloween, in his all-time favorite costume. (age four)

Homer at the tender age of ten. That's Barney Gumble on the left.

Dear Dad,
I'll do anything you say, just don't send me to military school. Please please please please please please please please. Your devotid son, Homer

P.S. Remember: Today is the first day of the rest of your life.

AWARD — Nice Try — WOODSHOP — FOR EFFORT

SIMPSON, H.

Homer's sophomore woodshop project — his first initial. He planned to finish the "J" as a junior and the "S" as a senior.

FROM THE DESK OF
Harlan Dondelinger

To: Abraham Simpson

From: Harlan Dondelinger
Vice Principal

Dear Mr. Simpson:
   I need to talk with you about ways to improve Homer's study habits. His constant efforts to draw attention to himself with noises imitating bodily functions and his off-color attempts at humor during class time have reached the point where I have no alternative but to warn you that drastic measures may be necessary. We've told him repeatedly that he's an underachiever, but Homer seems to think that's a compliment.

Sincerely,

Harlan Dondelinger
Vice Principal

← Yours truly!

Mrs. Harvell → 4th   SPRINGFIELD ELEMENTARY

Barney!

Mrs. Harvell

Principal Hartley

HANDWRITING ANALYSIS

Your Personality Revealed Through Penmanship!

SIGNATURE ___*Marge Bouvier*___

Your signature indicates a sensitive, free-spirited and creative nature. The graceful calligraphic curvatures of your capital letters reveal a love of poetry and music. You are destined for a life of elegance, refinement and artistic fulfillment.

SIGNATURE ___HOMER SIMPSON___

Your signature exhibits a strong tendency toward slackness, inattention and woolgathering. The unsophisticated arrangement of ill-formed lines and circles which comprise your writing suggests an obtuse and insipid outlook. You are doomed to a life of banality, dullness and lethargy.

ROSES ARE RED
Violets ARE
BLUE NO ONE
I KNOW
speaks FRENCH
AS BEAUTIFULLY
AS YOU.
L'AMOUR,
HOMER

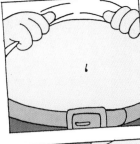

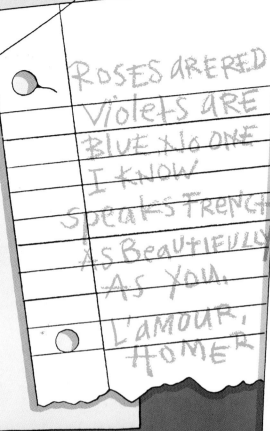

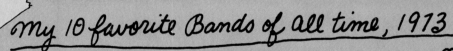

My 10 favorite Bands of All time, 1973

1. Ringo Starr
2. The Beatles
3. The Larry Davis Experience
4. The Happies
5. Elf Gravy
6. Don Donnally and Jo-Jo

7. Beatlemania
8. The Twigs of Sister Tomorrow
9. The Love Buckets
10. Mr. Funky and the Springfieldians

R.S. + M.B.

Homer's other love — his car ← Such fond memories!

You do your thing
And I'll do mine
Free to Be
You and Me
And if, by chance,
We find our Karma entwined,
With no strings attached,
Then that's the
Bag we are in.
With no hassles
Or commitments.

—Joshua

FROM "GUESS WHO"? (HOMER!)

Joshua was Homer's favorite male vocalist. I understand he sells real estate in California now.

SA0417 SEC 10 L 108 ADULT
EVENT CODE SECTION / AISLE ROW / BOX SEAT ADMISSION 10.50
10.50 ORCH DOOR 1
002.00

SPRINGFIELD AUDITORIUM
PRESENTS
THE GLOOMY MOODS
NO REFUNDS NO EXCHANGES
TUES. AUGUST 4,1974 8:15PM

I had a poster-sized version of this timeless sentiment, but it was damaged in my attempt to decoupage it onto a piece of driftwood

YOU AND ME
AND A DOG
NAMED "FREE"
(Dave Spammer)

THE
BLACKLIGHT
CRASHPAD
Produced by
Herb "Hip" Stevens

BENICERATA

GO BAREFOOT THROUGH THE LAWNS OF TIME NOT KNOWING THE SHARP THINGS THAT LIE ahead. Avoid hateful & negative people except if they are immediate family. Take heart. ☺ Speak not ill of others & listen not to other ill-speakers unless you are concealed. Consider that two wrongs do not a right make nor three a crowd. Whenever possible, think nice thoughts. Smile. ☺ Be comforted that in the darkest hour someone is getting some sleep. Strive at all times to leave a room brighter than when you entered it. Cheer up. ☺ You are a love child of Mother Earth & whether you know it or not, she really just wants what is best for you. Therefore, be mellow in your peevishness. Be not the Gloomy Gus nor the rain cloud that mopes from on high. Repel those who are dismal & glum as you yourself are shunned by those seeking a good time. ☺ Have a nice day.

AUTHOR UNKNOWN

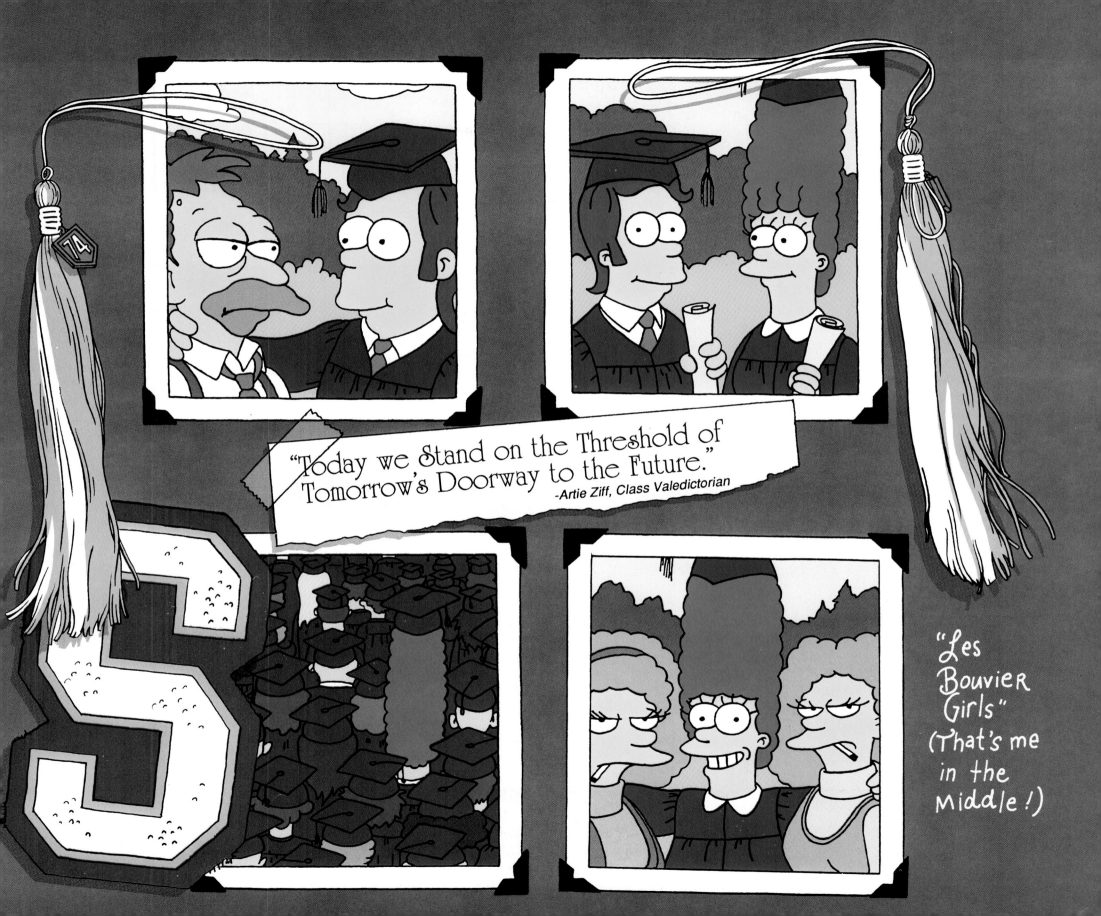

"Today we Stand on the Threshold of Tomorrow's Doorway to the Future."
-Artie Ziff, Class Valedictorian

"Les Bouvier Girls" (That's me in the Middle!)

Certificate of Mer[it]

THIS IS TO CERTIFY THAT

Marjorie Bouvier

has successfully completed the rigorous curriculum of th[e]
Springfield Unified School District and is hereby deeme[d...]

Excellent

Given this 16th Day of June,
Nineteen Hundred and 74.

Grace Vitale

Supervisor, Springfield Unified School District   Principal, Springfield High Sch[ool]

Certificate of Merit

THIS IS TO CERTIFY THAT

Homer Simpson

has successfully completed the rigorous curriculum of the
Springfield Unified School District and is hereby deemed...

Adequate

Given this 16th Day of June,
Nineteen Hundred and 74.

Grace Vitale

Supervisor, Springfield Unified School District   Principal, Springfield High School

Homer

The Annual
Senior Class
Graduation
Bonfire and
Weenie
Roast

Marriage Certificate

THIS DOCUMENT CERTIFIES ___Marge Bouvier___

AND ___Homer Simpson___ TO BE UNITED IN HOLY

MATRIMONY ON THE ___29___ DAY OF ___September___

BY THE POWERS VESTED (BY LAW) IN A JUSTICE OF THE

PEACE, AT THE ___Lucky 7 Wedding Chapel___

Milford A. Alexander
Justice of the Peace

OFFICIATED

Doris Troy
Clerk

"May your marriage not be a lemon."

Our favorite casino!
Such lovely
memories!

The
WOODEN
NICKEL
Saloon &
Casino

HEY-
WHAT HAVE
YOU GOT
TO LOSE?!

THE TOMB OF THE
UNKNOWN
HITCH-
HIKER

A Public Service Cautionary Statue

THIS COUPON ENTITLES
BEARER TO ONE (1)
FREE ALCOHOLIC
BEVERAGE OF CHOICE.
WITH PURCHASE OF $50 IN CHIPS.
Sorry: No Tropical Drinks,
Blended Drinks or Soft Drinks

For the Tub of Your Life
KUSTOM-KRAFTED
SPAS AND HOT TUBS
Nathen "Red" Wood
"Not 'Just Another' Spa & Hot Tub Salesman"
24 Hour Beeper: 1-800-555-9007

We met this nice
man while playing keno.
I found it hard to believe
he was in such a risqué
line of work!

This grim monument is located on a particularly
desolate stretch of highway not far from the Lucky 7.

DEAR Ringo,

I hope you like this paINTING I DID
oF you. You are my favorite musician in
the universe (really!)

What do you like to eat?
Is your hair really that shape all the time?
Do you have hamburgers and French fries
in England?

Well, that's all for now. Please write me
you have time in your very busy schedule.

Yours truly,

Your biggest fan,

Marge Bouvier ☺

Marge Bouvier

(P.S. I am
not a
lunatic.)

SPRINGFIELD
THIRD
PLACE
FAIR

Lucky Coin Gelatin Mold
(whoever gets the coin is Lucky for a day!)

2 packs blue gelatin mix

3 cups "Krusty Brand" corn
sweetener

1 lb. bag multi colored
"Kitchen Dee-Lite" miniature
marshmallows

1 Lucky coin (for chefs on a budget,
pennies are acceptable. For special
events, try using a Bicentennial
quarter.)

My secret ingredient:

: Fla

Boil gelatin i
Pour into m
Add marshm
Chill for

Voila!

SPRINGFIELD GELATIN COOK-OFF

BOUVIER

THIRD
PLACE

August 1980

For this prize-winning mold, I used an Indian-head nickel! ↑

CAREER OPPORTUNITIES
with the
Soon-to-Open
SPRINGFIELD NUCLEAR POWER PLANT

Your Future is Glowing!

HAVE A TALL, COOL ONE!

SPRINGFIELD NUCLEAR POWER PLANT

FREE SOUVENIR PLASTIC TUMBLERS TO OUR FIRST 500 JOB APPLICANTS!

"Radiating Good Will Throughout the Community."

SPRINGFIELD NUCLEAR POWER PLANT
EMPLOYEE EVALUATION SHEET

Complete the Sentence: The most important thing for any worker is: _____

to try NOT TO LET THE SAME SONG KEEP RUNNING THROUGH YOUR HEAD

Behind my back, friends say I'm: ~~AN EASY~~ ~~WORTH KNOWING~~ BRAVE, CLEAN AND REVEREND.

My ideal dinner would be: **APPROVED** Smothered WITH COUNTRY GRAVY.

Hom

page 12

S.N.P.P. IDENTIFICATION CARD   1976

NAME: SIMPSON, HOMER

CLASS: SECTOR D

00876-54779-4

Homer Simpson

OUR MOTTO: A Tense Workplace is a Productive Workplace

NUCLEAR POWER IS OUR BEST FRIEND

Homer on the morning of his first day of work as a Power Plant employee!

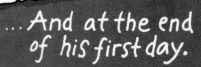
...And at the end of his first day.

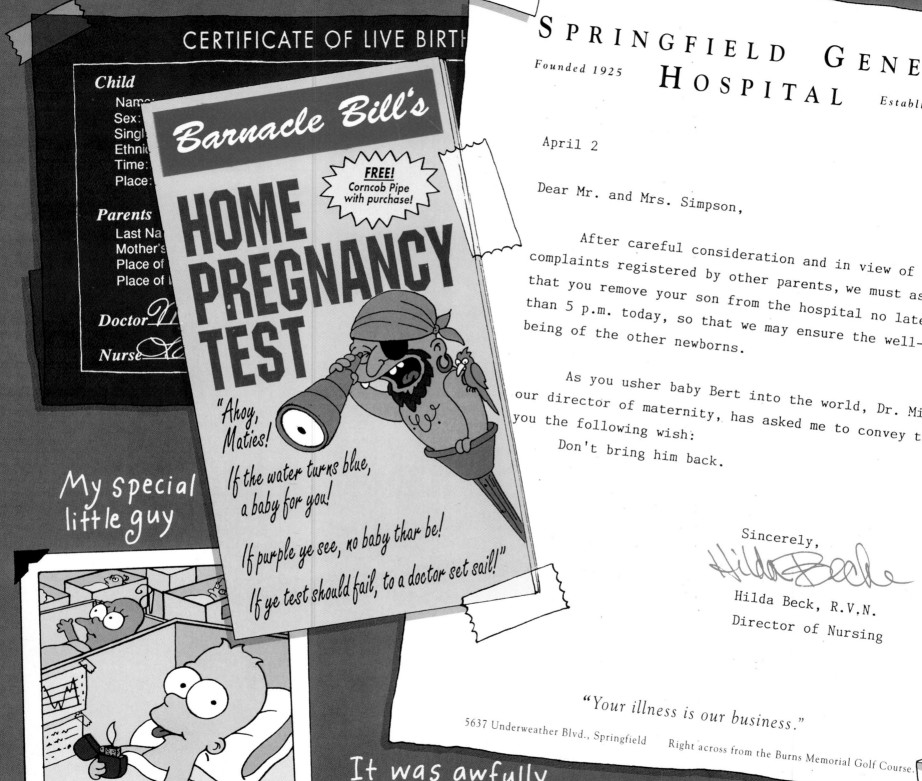

It's a BOY!

OK OUT, MOM!

Be Smart... Use BARTS Tactics

Bart's teething spoon

Here Comes TROUBLE

IT'S A BOY!

and he's OUT OF THIS WORLD!

We were so proud!
(And still are!)

New Arrivals

WELCOME
Justinian Toby Carson of Springfield. A robust 8 pounds 4 ounces of All-American Boy, and no April Fool! Congratulations from your gushing grandparents—Libby, Big Bill, Viv and Captain Jack.

AIN'T SHE SWEET?!
Ashley Tiffany Hurley Born March 30 to Joe Don and Raelene Hurley of Springfield. Younger than springtime by nine days, honey, but you'll catch up soon enough. From your cousins Jim Bob, Erlene and Buford of Capital City, where all of us Hurleys are in a real hurry to meet you.

TROUBLE AHEAD!
Bartholomew J. Simpson Born April 1 to Homer and Marjorie Simpson of Springfield. A mere 7 pounds 5 ounces of spon- taneous combustion, but look what that one little cow did to Chicago. Marge, don't say we didn't warn you. Your loving sisters are close by in case 911 is busy. Patty and Selma. P.S. We saw Artie Ziff the other day and he asked after you. Such a nice boy.

EGG DROP!
Huong Kim Nguyen Born April 2 to Nguyen and Thu Nguyen of Springfield. Especially for you, little Nguyen, a birthday haiku:

Lotus child, welcome.
It's a small world after all.
Springfield, have a cow!

From your auntie Kim Tran.

The Happy Family!

SPRINGFIELD GENERAL HOSPITAL

Name: Simpson, Bartholomew

Parents: Marge/Homer

Date: April 1st

Weight: 7.2 lbs.

Length: 19.0"   Sex: ✗ M

Delivering Physician:

Dr. Julius Hibbert

PATIENCE AND INSIGHT ARE NOT ~~IN~~ YOUR VOCABULARY ← Homer's

YOU ARE ABOUT TO UNDERTAKE A LONG AND THANKLESS TASK ← Mine

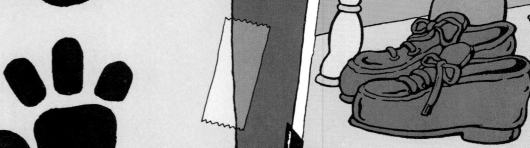

My first grey hair (and hopefully my last!)

SPRINGFIELD GENERAL HOSPITAL

CLAIMS DEPT.

We regret to inform you that unless the outstanding balance shown below is paid in full by September 15, we will have no alternative but to repossess your child.

Delivery and Maternity Care
Bartholomew J. Simpson
Balance Due: $1,499.99

FINAL NOTICE

BARTHOLOMEW J SIMP

I was so thrilled when the doctor announced:
"four toes on each foot, four fingers on each hand."

Bart and Lisa's first Haircuts.

Lisa's hair never quite grew back the same.

We spent
the night with

ELVISH

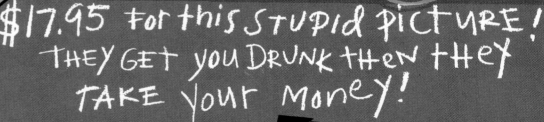

$17.95 for this STUPID PICTURE!
THEY GET YOU DRUNK THEN THEY
TAKE YOUR MONEY!

Homer at the slots.
He kept saying he "felt lucky", so I couldn't stop him.

Jackpot!

Homer after
he lost the entire
$ 11,158.97

Homer's Shining Hour

Needless to say, we could not afford to pay our bill.

These nice men wanted to take Homer for a ride, but I assured them it wasn't necessary.

We spent a few weeks more at the old Wooden Nickel than we'd planned.

Greetings from **POTATO ROCK**

NATIONAL PARK

A visit to our state's most wondrous rock formation

Homer doing "the Hustle" atop P.R.

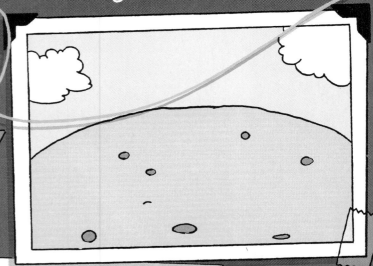

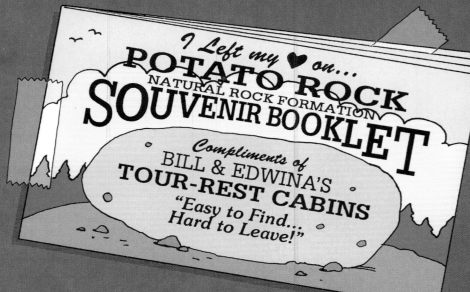

I left my ♥ on...
POTATO ROCK
NATURAL ROCK FORMATION
SOUVENIR BOOKLET

Compliments of
BILL & EDWINA'S
TOUR-REST CABINS
"Easy to Find...
Hard to Leave!"

He joked,
"Where's the
sour cream
and chives?"
just before
he fell off.

Homer was determined not to let this happen again. He bought a new "Liquid Center" ball in the pro shop right afterwards and couldn't wait to try it...

PARTYING DOWN!

Apu donated 76 lbs. of beef jerky to the cause!

Homer in Rare Form

NEW! Liquid Center BOWLING BALL Revolutionary Design lends "Gravitational Impact" to pins!

ON SALE NOW IN... *"The Pro Shop"* of Springfield Lanes

You Can't Get Enuff...

Armando's Saws OPEN 24 HOURS!

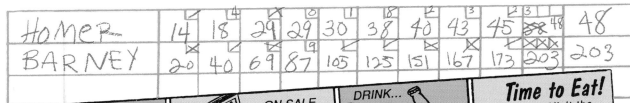

HOMER	14	18	29	29	30	38	40	43	45	48	48
BARNEY	20	40	69	87	105	125	151	167	173	203	203

THE STEALTH BOWLER NEW! THE PINS WON'T KNOW WHAT HIT 'EM!

ON SALE NOW IN... *"The Pro Shop"* of Springfield Lanes

DRINK... **Duff BEER** CAN'T GET ENUFF OF THAT WONDERFUL DUFF!

Time to Eat! Visit the Gutter-ball Lounge! OPEN 24 HRS.

HOMER	10	10	10	16	26	26	38	38	49	49	49
BARNEY	0	0	27	42	51	79	87	107	127	157	157

Lisa at 22 months.
Such a perceptive child!

Yet quite sensitive.

Family Xmas

Snowball I as a
kitten. She was
cute, but she was
BAD!

Springfield kindergarten
REPORT CARD

Name: <u>SIMPSON, LISA</u>
Teacher: <u>MRS. WELLSLEY</u>

Alphabet	A
Storytime	A
Cookies & Milk Time	A
	B
Recess	A
Songtime	A
Numbers	A

Mrs. Simpson,

Lisa is a bright and introspective child. The word "gifted" may be applicable. Although perhaps she is too introspective and gifted for her own good.

Mrs. Wellsley

BART - AGE 8

Bart's first black eye. (and not his last, I'm afraid.)

Lisa with her kindergarten teacher, Mrs. Wellseley. (And her baritone sax) Age 5.

I had a cat named
Snowball--
She died! She died!
Mom said she was
sleeping--
She lied! She lied!
Why oh why is my
cat dead?
couldn't that Chrysler
hit me instead?
- Lisa Simpson

Here I am pregnant with Little Maggie!

Maggie was such an easy child! By the time she came along, I knew all the tricks!

Maggie's First Birthday

EL BARTO WAS HERE

I was So, so, so proud! ↓

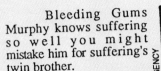
November 4, 1989

Murphy's Tenor Evokes Youthful Anxiety

By Jiff Johnson, *Shopper Music Critic*

Bleeding Gums Murphy knows suffering so well you might mistake him for suffering's twin brother.

Last night at the Jazz Hole, however, Springfield's resident jazzman extraodinaire bent the reed of his tenor sax in the direction of second grader Lisa Simpson.

Murphy introduced the 7-year-old Miss Simpson's composition "The Manipulative Daddy Blues" to an appreciative Hole audience.

What makes this collaboration work is the juxtaposition of Murphy's well-worn (but never tired) voice of experience with the stark, honest perception of Simpson's

youthful dilemma: the need to function in an oppressive home environment while simultaneously yearning for a liberated artistic space.

Murphy's quarte appearing indefinitely a Springfield's leading jaz venue, continues to brea new ground in this mo American of all music idioms.

proudly presents

BLEEDING GUMS MURPHY

and the

ART ENSEMBLE OF SPRINGFIELD

TONIGHT thru SUNDAY, 8am 'till Midnight
Sunday Morning "Breakfast Jazz Jam" 8-11am

To Lisa—
The hottest little sax player in town.
Your friend—
Bleeding Gums

DAVE NELSON

(You Must Say You Are at Least 21)

I don't know much about this man's music, but I do wish he'd do something about that Name!

Also Appearing

Nightly at the JAZZ HOLE...
MITZI McVEIGH
Oo-bop Sh-bam, she's Springfield's First Lady of Scat...
The sweet-sounding little soprano with the big, fast tounge!

The Day Homer Got His New Camera

Poem #254

"Optimism" is the thing with fur
That curls upon the sofa
And dreams of Happy Little
            Elves
And never snores -- at all

And in the grimmest hour
    is there --
And annoying though my family be
They cannot bestir the Gentle
            Beast
That keeps my spirit free.

So long I've nurtured it
And thus I'll be repaid.
For it shall, I know it shall
Bring a pony unto me.

            Lisa Simpson (age 7)

Maggie's First Step
(well, actually seconds
after her first step)

Maggie's second step

I didn't even know she had
a pet named "Optimism"!
I just hope it's not some
Sort of rodent.

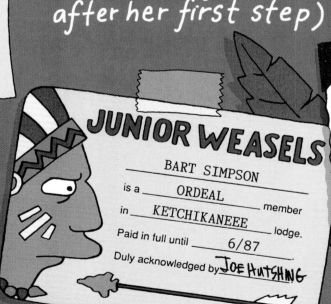

JUNIOR WEASELS

BART SIMPSON

is a _____ORDEAL_____ member

in _____KETCHIKANEEE_____ lodge.

Paid in full until _____6/87_____.

Duly acknowledged by JOE HUTSHNG

Bart's arrowhead, which he found
at Camp Itchawanda while hunting
for "snipes."

Luckily, Bart was
a lousy shot.

WARMEST Wishes for a Happy Mother's Day!

MAGGIE

BART

Lisa

COOK YOUR FAVORITE MEAL TONIGHT HONEY! LOVE, HOMER

My lovely Mother's Day card from my loving family...

And my Mother's Day gift from Homer. He explained that he truly believed it's the thought that counts. (Hmm.)

Dumb Things I Gotta Do Today...

Shopping List
1. frozen pork chops (Jumbo Pack)
2. Frosty Krusty Flakes
3. Happy Little Elf Cereal
4.
5.
6. 10 lb. bag of sugar
7. Gelatin Mix (12-pack)
11. Pork Rinds Lite
12. Stuff-itz
13. Kitty Krunchies
14. Yummy Cupcake Mix
15. Lard
16. Xtra-Gritty Peanut butter
17. Diet Brownies
18. Duff Beer (don't forget coupon!)
19.

SPRINGFIELD RETIREMENT CASTLE

To; Advertisers
KLMP Tv
Springfield

DEAR Advertisers,
   I am disgusted with the way old people are depicted on television. We are not all vibrant, fun-loving sex maniacs. Many of us are bitter, resentful individuals who remember the good olddays when entertainment was bland and inoffenseive. The following is a list of words I never want to hear on television again. Number one; Bra. Number two; Horny. Number three; Family jewels.

Sincerely yours,
Abraham Simpson
Grandpa Simpson

Grandpa strikes again!

Memories of a vacation Homer would like to forget

greetings from,
THE DEVIL'S HELL HOLE

SLIPPERY WHEN WET

THE HOTTEST SPOT IN THE USA!

Patty and Selma said the resorts of the Devil's Hell-Hole region are the playgrounds of the rich and famous. But I can't imagine rich people wanting to be so darned uncomfortably hot and sweaty!

89¢

GENUINE! DEVIL'S HELL-HOLE SAN

IT IS A FEDERAL OFFENSE TO REMOVE THIS POSTER FROM PUBLIC WALLSPACE!

WANTED

ARTIST RENDERINGS DRAWN FROM WITNESS DESCRIPTIONS

FOR DEFACEMENT OF PUBLIC PROPERTY

Alias: *El Barto*

Name: *Unknown*

Height: *Approx. 6'3"*

Weight: *Approx. 248 lbs.*

Distinguishing Marks: *None*

TO PROTECT
SPRINGFIELD
POLICE
DEPT
AND SERVE

Description: Suspect is wanted for wantonly spray painting "El Barto" in cursive script on numerous buildings in and around Springfield.

Suspect has been sighted carrying slingshot in back pocket and should be considered dangero Observers also warn that if confronted by suspect, citizens should not, under any circunstance engage suspect in verbal conflict. However, if helpful phrases are needed to keep suspect at b notify Springfield police by dialing 1-800-HEY-COPS.

I certainly hope they find him! Where would we be if everybody wrote their names wherever they wanted?

Dr. Marvin Monroe

FAMILY THERAPY

AS SEEN ON TV!

IT REALLY WORKS!

YES! We have Aggression Therapy Mallets!

I don't remember the specific occasion, but it was a lovely card! →

With deepest Sympathy in your dark time of Disgrace and Mortification

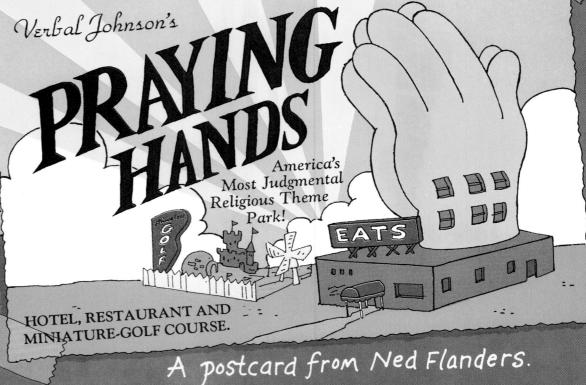

Verbal Johnson's

PRAYING HANDS

America's Most Judgmental Religious Theme Park!

GOLF

EATS

HOTEL, RESTAURANT AND MINIATURE-GOLF COURSE.

A postcard from Ned Flanders.

Greetings from SPRINGFIELD

Home of the Springfield Nuclear Power Plant!

In hopes of a profitable New Year—

I'm watching you.
C. Montgomery Burns

Homer's Car!

HOMER SIMPSON

SPRINGFIELD ISOTOPES

MASCOT

DANCIN' HOMER SIMPSON

Took the baseball world by surprise in May 1990 when his spontaneous "Baby Elephant Walk" routine during Family Night became the talk of Springfield... Popular appeal earned him a shot at the majors, but "Walk" failed to catch on with Capital City fans...Among mascots, shares record (with several others) for shortest major league career.

HEIGHT: 5'9" **WT:** 239 lbs. **AGE:** 35

LITTLE KNOWN FACT: Homer was named Springfield Nuclear Power Plant "Toxic Waste Handler of the Month" in November, 1986.

"KEEP ONE EYE... ON THE OTHER GUY."

PEER OBSERVATION PROGRAM

OFFENDING EMPLOYEE: _Homer Simpson_
DATE OF OFFENSE: _8-4-85_
TIME OF OFFENSE: _All Day_

Feel free to check as many offenses as you like. Every effort will be made to keep accuser's name confidential, but management cannot be responsible for leaked information.

EMPLOYEE HAS BEEN SEEN OR HEARD:

✓ taking a nap of more than 15 minutes while opperationg equipment

✓ taking fissionable matieral home for personal use

✓ taking Mr. Burns' name in vain

✓ taking liberties

✓ other (use back of card to describe)

SIGNED (optional): _Anonymous_

Thank you for helping make the plant more productive.

(Please do not fill out this form on company time.)

A Simpson on a trading card — I never thought I'd see the day!

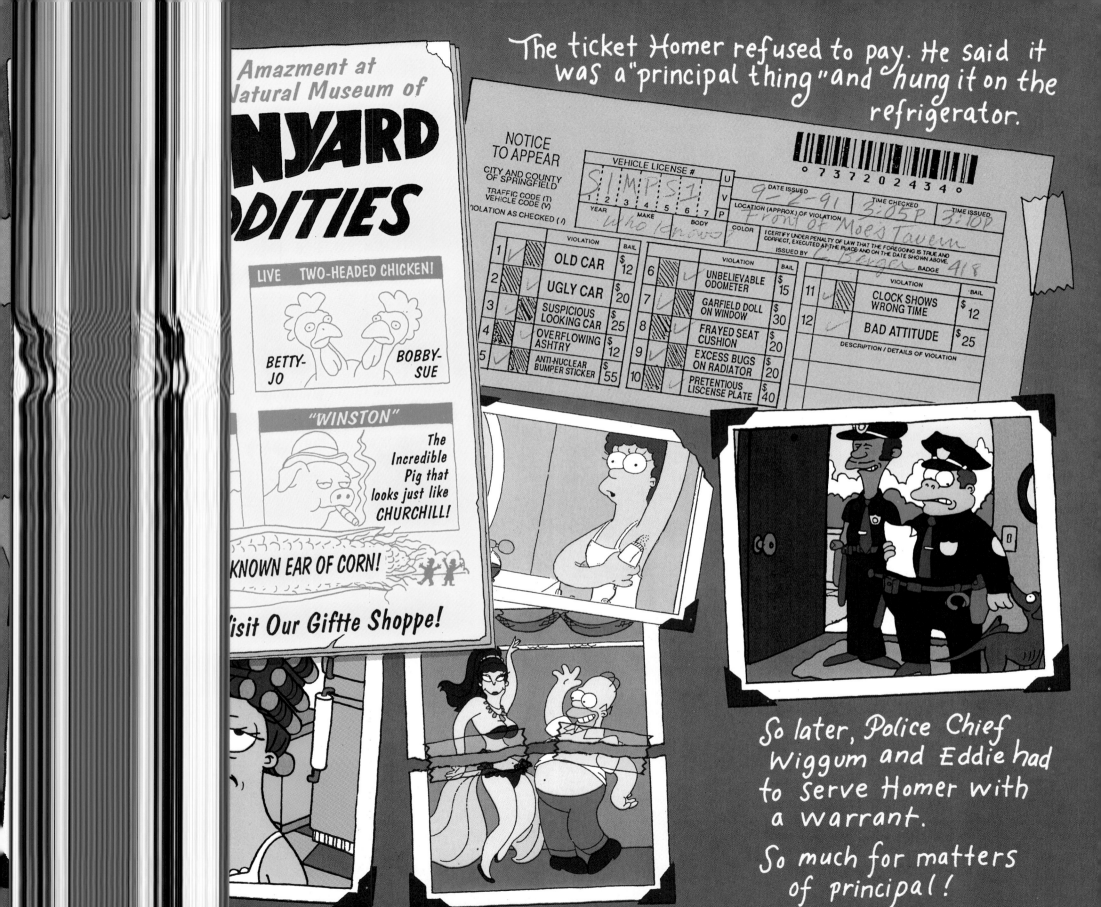

The ticket Homer refused to pay. He said it was a "principal thing" and hung it on the refrigerator.

So later, Police Chief Wiggum and Eddie had to serve Homer with a warrant.

So much for matters of principal!

Needless to say, it bounced.

Bart's tattoo. What a frightening experience! We had it removed immediately.

Ned and Maude F. sent us this one. On the back it reads: "Pray for peace, prepare for war, and vicey-versa!" That certainly is food for thought!

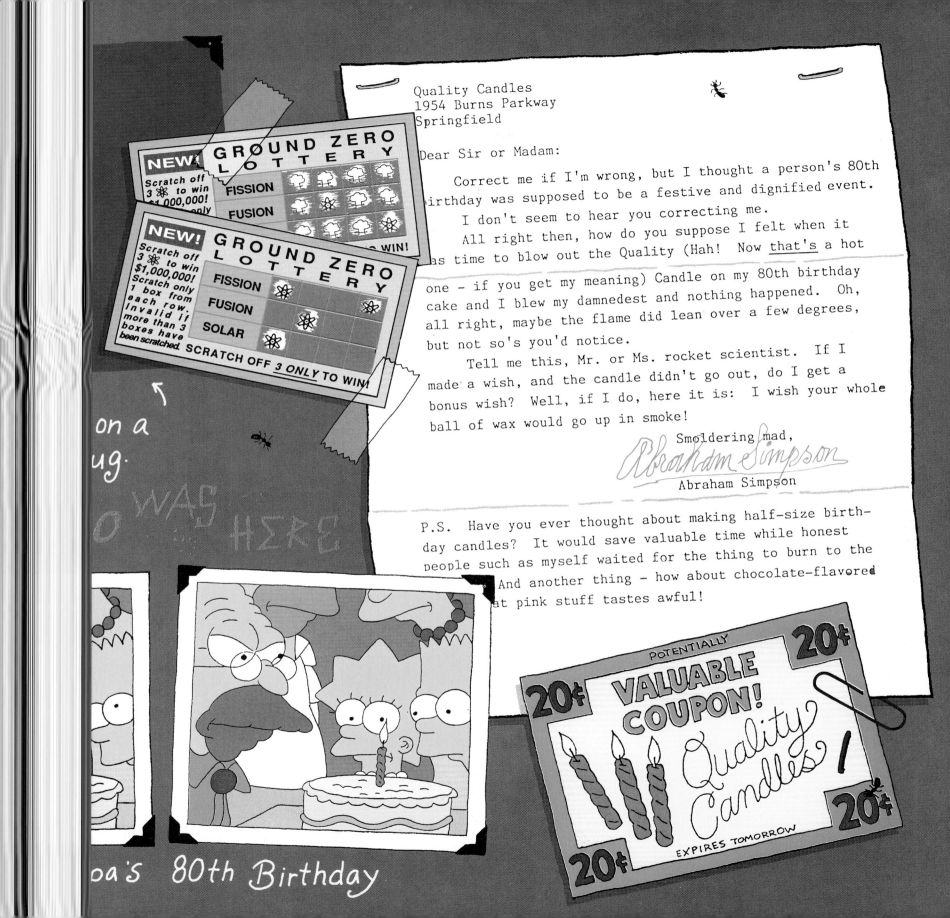

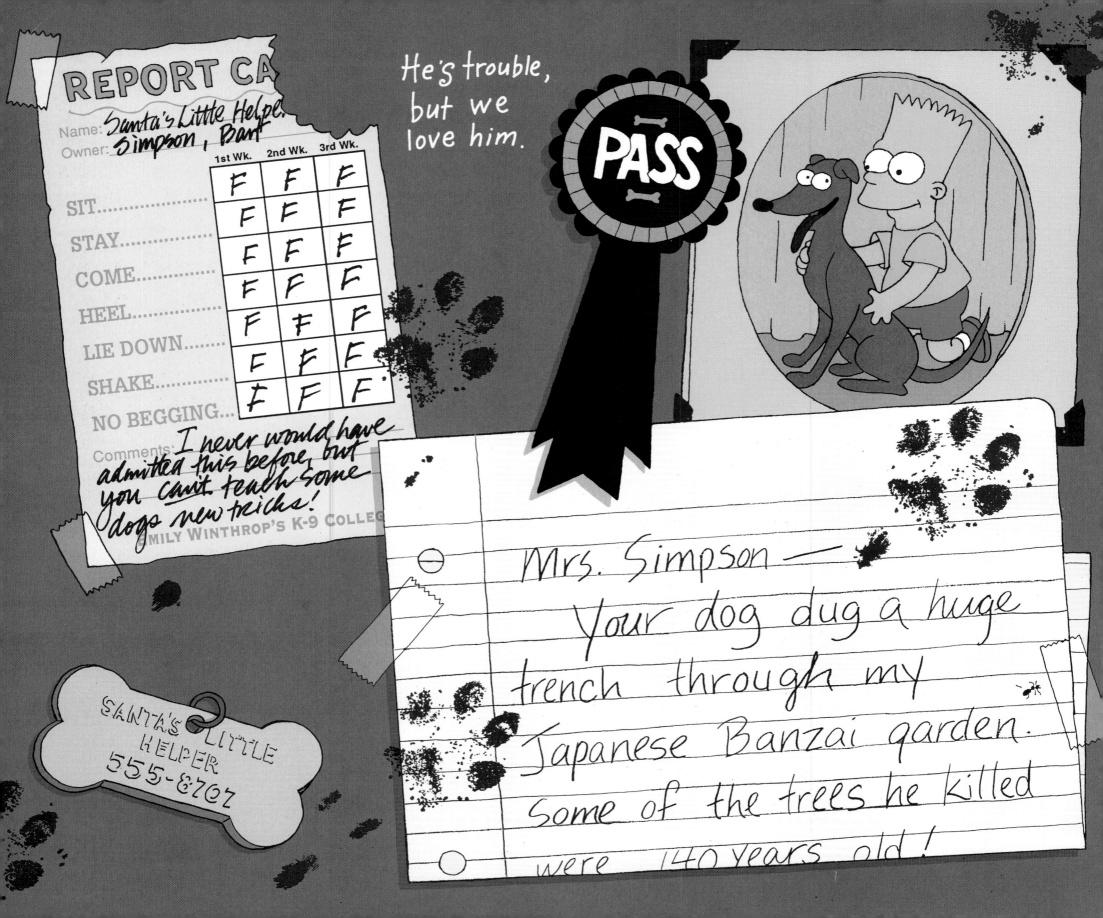

ELD RETIREMENT CASTLE

KING OAK DRIVE, SPRINGFIELD

April 14

e no intention of reading a single word
," but in my day if a book like that
s it would last about five minutes.

saying that all the copies would be
f smut-thirsty lowlifes but if you DO
ying, you are sadly mistaken my friends,
ike "And Then They Took Naps" would be
by the proper authorities and would never

ike a bunch of muskrats in a monsoon
st Admendment argument and trying to
of speech line, let me remind you that in
of putting Springfield women's or any
bewteen the covers of a book or between a
tter.

only lead to blowing the cover of MEN'S
r real-life misdeeds, and you wouldn't wa
E my own little indiscretion with a woman
This is the sort of thing nobdy would a
eir deathbed, which is exactly what I did
and ask yourself, "What would I do?"

Sincere

ING BUT A SNOOZER!

es, *Shopper Book Editor*

Then They Took Naps", a
novel based on the fantasy
lives of certain Springfield
er)   housewives.
The session was lively
est at   and sometimes heated. An
nthly   argument broke out when
gfield   Selma Bouvier stood up and
e was   interrupted Ms. Lovejoy,
uthor   saying, "Well, let's stop
f our   pussy-footing around, shall
we? I mean, just who *are* the
from   housewives you describe in
,"And   'Naps'?"

Ms. Bouvier's challenge
touched off a raucous
argument among the 23
members present, half of
whom joined her call for full
disclosure, chanting, "Let's
hear the names!"

Chairperson Marjorie
Simpson finally restored
order by shouting above the
noise,"Ladies! Please! I think
we can agree there's a little
of all of us in every one of
these characters. Now, isn't it

about time for the
lovely cookies
baked for us today
by Gloria Blaze,
uh, I mean Maude
Flanders…"?

Next month's
meeting will
welcome the
much-traveled
botanist and
photographer
Lee Maltborn, who will
discuss his highly acclaimed

HOUSEWIFE WEEKLY

Beauty Tips Contest!

SIMPLY FILL OUT THE FORM BELOW WITH ALL YOUR FAVORITE, TRIED-AND-TRUE BEAUTY SECRETS! WE ALL HAVE OUR LITTLE MIRACLE FORMULAS AND TOP-SECRET WRINKLE REMEDIES TO KEEP US LOOKING GOOD, SO WHY NOT SHARE YOURS?

1. ~~To remove wrinkles, sleep with a yogurt facial treatment. Be sure to stir up fruit~~ from bottom!

2. To make your eyes look bigger, curl lashes.

3. When in doubt about your hair, tease it!

4. Always clench your teeth when you smile.

5. Gravity is Beauty's enemy number one. Maintain bouyant thoughts

6. For younger-looking skin, lie face down in a mud puddle

7. for 20 minutes. Mix your base with orange food coloring for a more "natural" look.

8. Keep your hair looking peppy with static electricity!

9. Instead of drying your hair with a blow dryer, ~~use a~~ cotton candy machine.

10. My number one beauty secret a wee...

YOU COULD WIN AN ALL-EXPENSE PAID TRIP TO HOUSEWIFE WEEKLY'S BEAUTY HEAD-QUARTERS, A COMPLETE MAKE-OVER AND AN OPPORTUNITY TO BE A "BEFORE" AND "AFTER" MODEL IN THIS MAGAZINE!

Name Ma___
Address ___
Wat___
Spring___
Zip 002__
Phone 555___

I almost sent this in, but the idea of being a "before" just rubbed me the wrong way.

Something about the father's disappearance left me with an uneasy sense of déjà-vu.

Snowball II, on the other hand, seemed completely unconcerned.

QUIRREL HOLLOW

AY IN TWO ACTS

he *Springfield Elementary Players*

berry..............................	Janey Hagstrom
berry..............................	Lewis Jackson
....	Susan Hegarty
....	Robert DuRee
aloney..............................	Frank Isola
....	Lisa Simpson
....	Bart Simpson
....	Nelson Widmar
....	Milhouse Light and Magic
....	Carin Berger
....	Terry Castillo
....	Mrs. Hoover

when Grandma finds her *go-to-meetin'* dress
s. On Grandpa's advice, she suspects Rufus
ut Rufus has a darn good alibi. Together,
and Rufus vow to get to the bottom of this.

ads straight to Ol' Bugeared Maloney—or does
t a darn good alibi too. Ol' Bugeared joins the
r vigilantes keep trying to get to the bottom of
a! (Hang onto your seats.)

AZZ
HOLE
presents
EEDING GUMS
MURPHY

Just Hats
Just the place
to just top off the outfit that's just
perfect for just about any occasion!
*Just off the Interstate at the corner of Burns
Parkway and Wiggum Ave. Dial 555-JUST*

Bart drew this at age seven...

She was so proud to be cast as the Mayor!

MY DAD
BART

Not a ↑ bad likeness, really.

Bart was in charge of lighting

At long last! One of Grandpa's letters finally gets published!

Our trip to Mt. Rushmore!

OCT. 2, 1989   SPRINGFI

SICK AND TIRED

Editor, *Springfield Shopper,*

I am sick and tired of writing angry, blathering letters to you morons and never seeing them in print!

Do you think I do this just to heart myself squawk?

The First Amendment should stand for more than just wasted stationery— paper doesn't grow on trees, you know!

—Grampa Simpson

FEBRUARY 9, 1990

Man nearly Dies in Bizarre Leap over Springfield Gorge

Another 10 ft. and he'd have made it.

Instead, dozens watched in horror as local resident Homer Simpson crashed and fell into the rocky depths of Springfield Gorge yesterday afternoon sail impromptu attempt across the familiar landmark on his son's skateboard.

GET WELL SOO

One of the greatest inventions since the t.v.!

BARTO WAS here

Recipes

PLAN-AHEAD, MAKE-AHEAD CALIFORNIA DIP

1 package onion soup mix
1/2 pint sour cream
Mix.
Chill.
Serve, with Krinkle-Time Potato Chips.

"Howl of the Unappreciated"
by Lisa Simpson

I saw the best meals of
my generation
destroyed by the madness
of my brother.
My soul carved in slices
by spikey-haired demons.

[k]sgiving Cranberry Log

2 cans xtra-jellied
seedless cranberry
sauce
Mint

Open cranberry jellies.
Place (tandem) on
decorative platter.
(be sure to slide out
carefully so jelly remains
in shape of can!)

Add "mint" for "leaves."
Voila!

El Bandito Motel

The year we decided to break with
Thanksgiving tradition and serve pork
chops instead!

with apologies
to the pilgrims.
—L.S.

Lisa's
lovely
cornucopia
centerpiece

SPRINGFIELD ELEMENTARY SCHOOL

March 6

Dear Mr. and Mrs. Simpson:

I know I've said this many times before, but this really is the last straw.

Enclosed you will find your son Bartholomew's latest pathetic attempt at forgery. If he thinks he can hoodwink my authority, he's got another think coming.

I'm afraid your son Bartholomew is on a one-way conveyor belt to J.D.H., and I don't mean the Junior Disneyland Hotel. I mean the Juvenile Detention Home!

I am adding another 40 days detention, which brings his total to 462 days.

He will also be required to write on the blackboard 1000 times:

A FORGED EXCUSE IS INEXCUSABLE.

I can only hope you will take even sterner measures of discipline in the privacy of your own home.

Sincerely,

Seymour Skinner

Seymour Skinner
Principal

REPORT CARD
SPRINGFIELD ELEMENTARY SCHOOL

Student: *Simpson, Bart*

	1st SEM.	2nd SEM.	3rd SEM.
Arithmatic	F	D-	F
Social Studies	D+	F	F+
English	D-	F+	D
History	F	F	D-
Art	F-	D	D+
P.E.	D+	F	F

Comments: *Dear Mr. and Mrs. Simpson, As we are painfully aware, Bart is his own worst enemy. Unfortunately, the enemy is winning. Nothing you or I could say or do would make a bit of difference.*

With mutual concern,
Ms. Krabappel

Age: *10*

...ilits need to
...on to himself.
...n includes
...n intended to
...nes and
...order.
...Park.
Loren Pryor

EL BARTO WAS HERE

SPRINGFIELD ELEMENTARY
GRADE FOUR
Ms. Krabappel

Ms. Krabappel   Principal Skinner

Merry Xmas!

Maggie

Snowball II

BART

Santa's Little Helper

Lisa

The Simpsons

Homer

Marge

QUICK RECIPE #3

1 MINUTE EGGNOG

Rum (1 pint)

Milk (1 quart)

Eggs (6)

Pour ingredients into a
blender, frappe 30 seconds
and serve at room temperatu
(*For housewives on the go—
make ahead of time and chill.*)

YULE LOG

1 pkg. Yellow Cake Mix
1 can Brown Frosting
Coffee can
gumdrops
parsley

Make cake mix. Pour into
coffee can. Bake 40 min.
Pull out of can (*important!*)
and frost.

Decorate with gumdrops.

Add parsley for "moss."

My Xmas List
Homer

- Stealth Bowler
- Coupon Booklet
  For Barney's
  Bowlarama
- NO TIES, please
- Case of Duff
- Mambo Refresher Course

list

what
get a

Merry Xmas from the
DEPARTMENT OF MOTOR VEHICLES
Free Ice Scraper to all Organ Donors before December 31st. (Limit 1 per customer).

My Xmas List
BART

tattoo - secret
         combo
         padlock
         for my
         bedroom
         door.
yoyo
ucer - MOON
ot   Shoes
um - Electric
       RAZOR
rra - RADIO
ull active Man
         walkie
rusty talkie
t-shirt
pace Mutants -
POP GUN

, 6:03 A.M.

Xmas morning, 6:07 A.M.

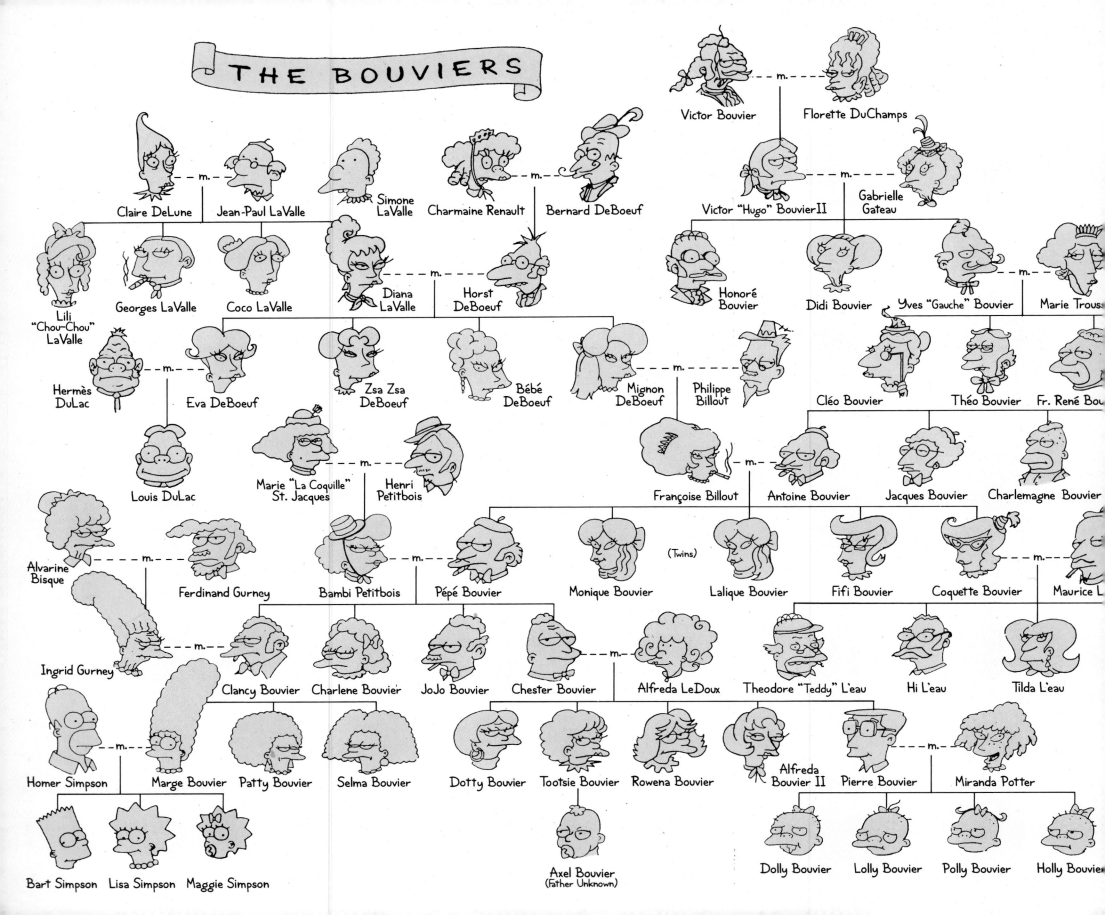

THE BOUVIERS